MW00623862

Monster Etiquette

An illustrated guide
for monsters, gargoyles, aliens, and nephews.

FIFTY PRINCIPLES TO HELP YOU

SECURE A RESPECTED PLACE

IN POLITE SOCIETY.

Manners are a sensitive awareness of the feelings of others.
If you have that awareness, you have good manners,
regardless of what fork you use.

EMILY POST (1872 – 1960)

Written and illustrated by Don Moyer
so he'd have a legitimate excuse to draw ridiculous creatures farting.

Published by Calamity Worldwide LLC
612 Pennridge Road, Pittsburgh, PA 15211
www.calamityware.com

Calamity number PT094
ISBN: 978-0-578-43719-4

First edition: May 2019
Printed and bound by inky wizards in China.

The world would be a better place if everyone behaved.

Sadly, many young creatures grow up without adequate opportunities to learn what constitutes good behavior in polite society. As a result, we are surrounded by loud, smelly, selfish, rude slubberdegullions. Let's do something about it.

In this book, you'll find a catalog of etiquette principles to help the ill-mannered behave with civility and grace. Pictures are included to make these ideas vivid and memorable.

If you are uncouth, these lessons will help you change their behavior. And, if you are already couth, reviewing these principles will give you a hoity-toity sense of superiority.

DISCLAIMER

The advice in this book is intended to help you behave in a civil manner. But the author bears no responsibility whatsoever for what happens when you apply these suggestions in the real world. As always, you are on your own. If you are jostled by fate, don't blame the advice in this book and don't blame the author.

Encounters

Relationships prosper,
out of the gate,
if you are thoughtful
and considerate.

Make a good start.

Reduce confusion for folks you talk to.
Make introductions. Explain who is who.

Grasp appendages firmly.

A handshake with no vigor (flaccid or limp),
marks you as a pipsqueak, untrustworthy wimp.

Step back.

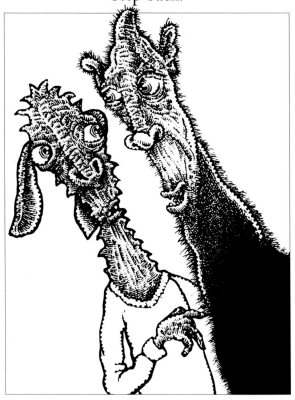

Never crowd strangers or touch private places.
Stay back. Keep out of personal spaces.

No smoking.

Want to start smoking? Ask for permission,
before exposing folks to noxious emissions.

Scatter no contagion.

*Cover your face when you cough or you sneeze
to block the spread of infectious disease.*

Don't hog the armrests.

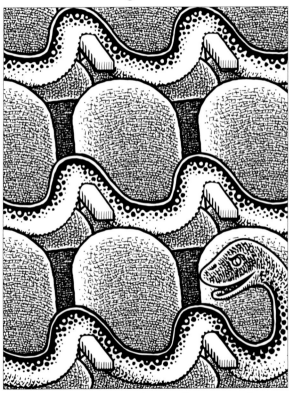

When you're in places where stuff's meant to share,
take pains to be sure you're not being unfair.

Hush.

As polite creatures know, bawling's repelling.
Express yourself, please, without howling or yelling.

8

Don't ogle.

It's rude to stare at boobs and private places.
Lift your gaze out of crotches. Look into faces.

Conversations

Make a gracious exchange—
of opinions and facts.
Join in. Help it flow.
Pick up the slack.

9

Don't bore.

Being stuck on one topic makes you a bore.
Find things to discuss—half a dozen or more.

Make eye contact.

Talking needs eye contact, so connections can grow.
Don't stare into space or at your gizmo.

Don't butt in.

Except for emergencies, it's considered disgusting.
Wait for a pause. Avoid interrupting.

Don't digress.

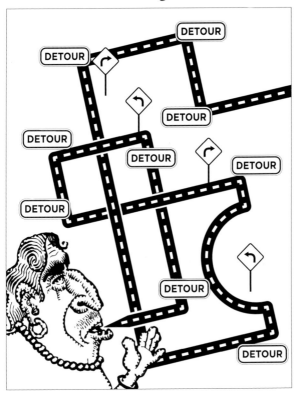

Talking with wild leaps is sure to disjoint.
Stay on topic and stick to your point.

Don't mumble.

Speak loudly. Speak clearly. Enunciate.
Slow down a bit so you don't obfuscate.

Avoid rude profanities.

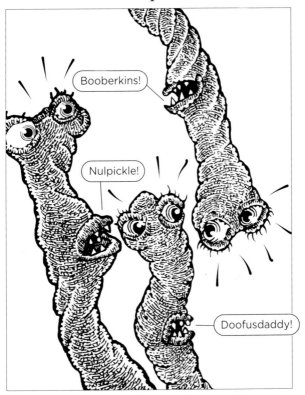

Harsh language and curses—best to eschew.
A bad reputation's hard to undo.

15

Use simple terms your listener knows.

By pushing the envelope, we deliver enhanced user experiences and monetize our core competencies.

No fancy terms, Don't attempt to dazzle.
Stick with plain words. Skip jargon and babble.

Don't discuss indelicate topics.

Don't talk body functions nor carnal cravings.
Skip how much you earn and how much you're saving.

Deportment

*Being pleasant to be with
is your number one goal.
Achieving it takes a
little self-control.*

Avoid offensive exhalations.

*Clearly ill-mannered to belch around neighbors,
breathe fire, spit, or expel noxious vapors.*

Avoid offgassing.

Emitting fumes is sure to appall.
The one polite smell is no smell at all.

19

Walk with grace.

Fix your slouch and shuffle and lazy rate.
Stand erect and abandon your slovenly gait.

Preserve tranquility.

Silence is golden. It's one of life's joys.
It's rude to blast others with your ghastly noise.

Don't fidgit.

Refined creatures don't need to wriggle.
They sit still or move slowly, little by little.

Dress for success.

Want to avoid an awkward episode?
Inquire in advance about the dress code.

Don't flirt.

*An innocent tease? Others might see
a rude, objectionable intimacy.*

No open displays of affection.

Hide amorous romantic contact, please.
In public no more than a pat or a squeeze.

Maintain hygiene.

Failing to keep clean offends everyone.
Don't make your reputation "slubberdegullion."

Don't whistle

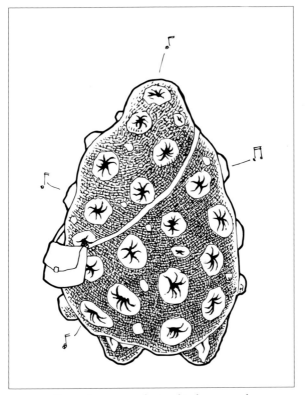

Genteel creatures don't whistle or growl.
They also forego the honk, hum, and howl.

Meals

Dining with others
is a basic action.
Behaving with care
stamps out all infractions.

Use the right implements.

*Observing companions can help you deduce,
in moments of doubt, which utensils to use.*

Don't monopolize the goodies.

Staking your claim to a comestible,
marks you as rude—wholly detestable.

Conceal the action.

Grace at your meals you will demonstrate,
if you close your mouth when you masticate.

Don't be a noisy eater.

At table, diners use only their voices,
and always refrain from making rude noises.

No double dipping.

When any food item's been up to your lips,
make sure it doesn't go back near the dips.

Share the last serving.

Playing hog is a serious matter.
Never snarf up the last treat on a platter.

Visits

*Making a visit
to where someone dwells?
Better show off behavior
that truly excels.*

Respond promptly to every RSVP.

Hostess is wondering if you'll attend.
Send your reply fast, so suspense will end.

Arrive on time.

It's extremely rude to make others wait.
Be on time or send word if you're running late.

Bring a gift.

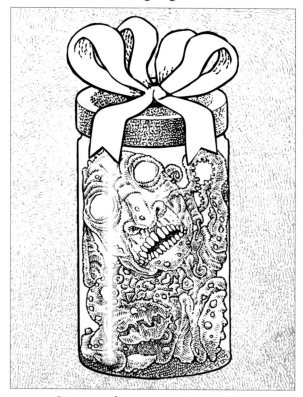

Bring your host a present, just a token.
To show him or her your couth is not broken.

Don't presume familiarity.

Remain aloof from the house's kids and pets.
Being too familiar leads to regrets.

Resist enhancements.

Good guests don't modify, alter, or tune.
Don't tweak, adjust, or rearrange the room.

Don't explore.

Don't snoop around on your own volition.
Before poking in rooms, ask permission.

Don't take things without permission.

Never help yourself to someone's stuff.
That's the same as theft. Critics will be rough.

Send thank-you notes promptly.

Your host has been generous, so don't be rude.
Write in a flash to express gratitude.

Integrity

*By your actions you
attract or disgust.
Make sure you're worthy
of everyone's trust.*

Say "Please."

You'll never go wrong if you add this expression.
Requests that skip it make a bad impression.

Say "Thank you."

Do you want to demonstrate how to be rude?
Just forget to express your gratitude.

Don't mock cherished beliefs.

Show respect and courtesy, just like you should,
on views of religion or what looks good.

Exhibit modesty.

Bragging on triumphs will irritate.
You make it worse when you exaggerate.

Don't take undeserved credit.

*You're stepping outside of the etiquette zone,
when you take credit for work not your own.*

Care for what you borrow.

Justify trust and make it your mission—
return everything in tip-top condition.

Never betray a confidence.

Trust is mangled, if secrets you reveal.
So, do not gossip. It just ain't genteel.

Demonstrate humility when you win.

Do not flaunt your win. Part of it was luck.
Show modesty. Don't be a mega-schmuck.

Don't whine when you lose.

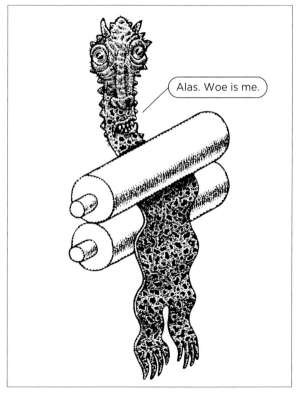

Losses will come. Don't excuse or complain.
Accept defeat with grace, despite the pain.

Apologize.

To avoid all mistakes would flabbergast.
Be quick with regrets. Say you're sorry, fast.

The journey begins

Of course, there's more to polite behavior than the 50 tips in this little book. I haven't even mentioned your curtsy or when to doff your hat. But the lessons included here will get you started on the etiquette path. Review this advice often to help make this behavior habitual. Even a monster can behave with refinement and grace.

Don
Pittsburgh, February 2019

Acknowledgements

Special thanks for the brilliant help provided by Karen Moyer, George Heidekat, Lynnette Kelley, Jack Kelley, and Doris Zurawka.

Author

Don Moyer is a retired graphic designer with the freedom to indulge in self-inflicted projects, like this. He draws a little every day. Don says, "I love to draw and the drawings I like best make me laugh." Don lives in Pittsburgh with The Amazing Karen.

Beautiful, useful, and funny

This book is one of the peculiar projects that emerged from the drawings in Don's sketchbooks. He's completed dozens of these efforts on Kickstarter and hopes to do many more. Discover more of these projects at www.calamityware.com, including Calamityware porcelain, fully-infested playing cards, letterpress prints, jigsaw puzzles, silks, BADbandanas, and the world's most charming shower curtain.

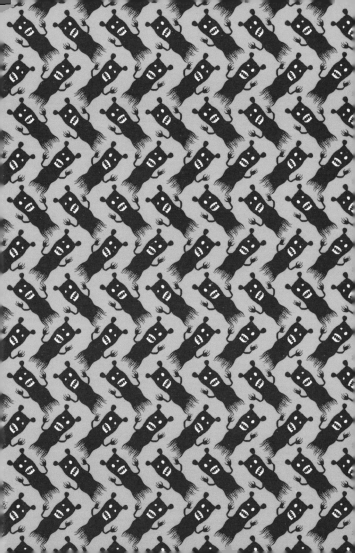

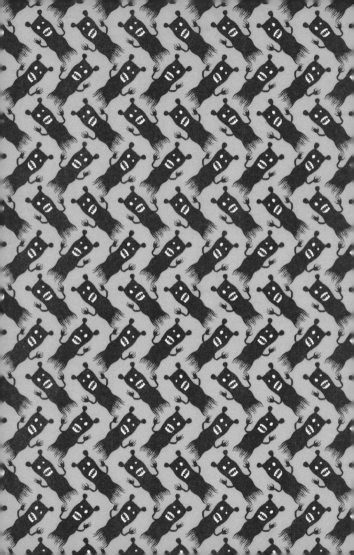